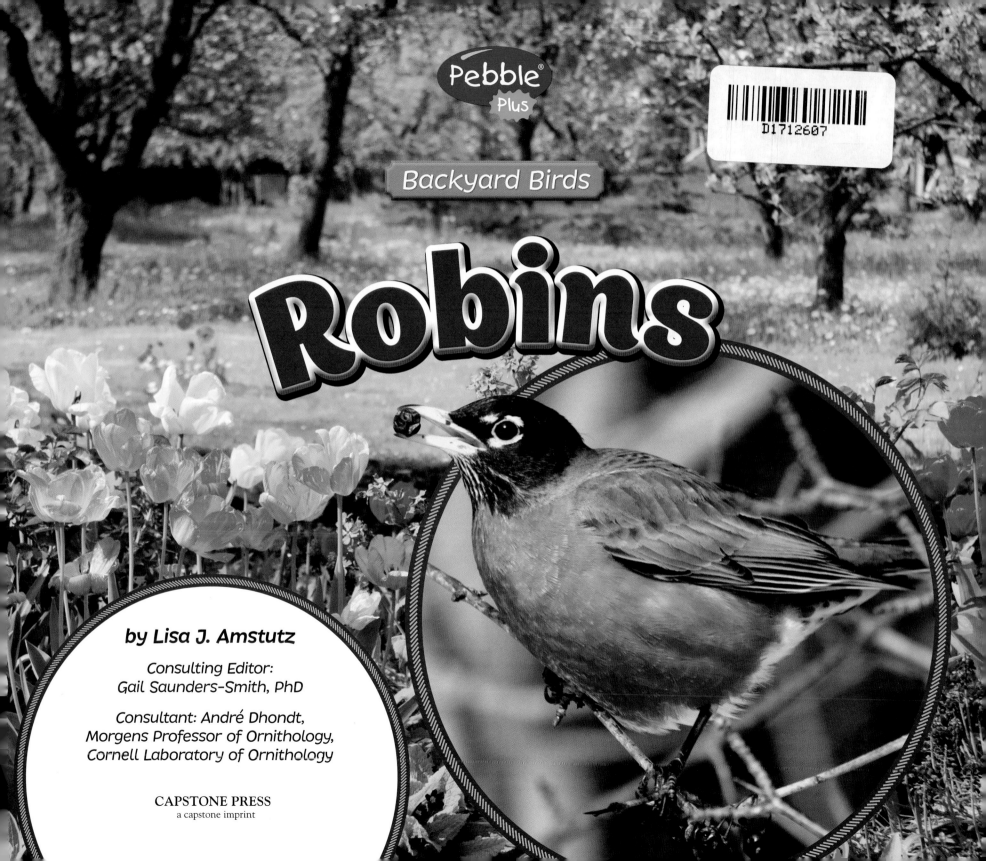

Pebble® Plus

Backyard Birds

Robins

by Lisa J. Amstutz

Consulting Editor:
Gail Saunders-Smith, PhD

Consultant: André Dhondt,
Morgens Professor of Ornithology,
Cornell Laboratory of Ornithology

CAPSTONE PRESS
a capstone imprint

Pebble Plus is published by Capstone Press,
1710 Roe Crest Drive, North Mankato, Minnesota 56003
www.capstonepub.com

Library of Congress Cataloging-in-Publication Data
Amstutz, Lisa J.
  Robins / by Lisa J. Amstutz.
     pages cm. — (Pebble plus. Backyard birds)
  Audience: Age 5-7.
  Audience: K to Grade 3.
  Summary: "Simple text and full-color photographs introduce American robins"—Provided by
publisher.
  Includes bibliographical references and index.
  ISBN 978-1-4914-6110-5 (library binding)
  ISBN 978-1-4914-6114-3 (paperback)
  ISBN 978-1-4914-6118-1 (eBook PDF)
  1. American robin—Juvenile literature. I. Title.
  QL696.P288A47 2016
  598.8'42—dc23   2015001329

Editorial Credits
Elizabeth R. Johnson, editor; Bobbie Nuytten, designer;
Svetlana Zhurkin, media researcher; Tori Abraham, production specialist

Photo Credits
Alamy: Mircea Costina, 19; Dreamstime: Dskow3, 9, Misscanon, 21, Petar Kremenarov, 7;
Shutterstock: Anatoliy Lukich, 5, Andre Helbig, cover (back), 1 (back), 2—3, 24, Anne Kitzman,
13, Chris Hill, cover (inset), 1 (inset), D and D Photo Sudbury, 15, Elliotte Rusty Harold, 11, Ivan
Kuzmin, 17, rvika, 4 and throughout

Note to Parents and Teachers

The Backyard Birds set supports national curriculum standards for science related to
life science and ecosystems. This book describes and illustrates American robins. The
images support early readers in understanding the text. The repetition of words and
phrases helps early readers learn new words. This book also introduces early readers
to subject-specific vocabulary words, which are defined in the Glossary section. Early
readers may need assistance to read some words and to use the Table of Contents,
Glossary, Read More, Internet Sites, Critical Thinking Using the Common Core, and
Index sections of the book.

Printed in the United States of America in North Mankato, Minnesota.
032018   000015

Table of Contents

All About Robins

Cheerily! Cheery!

A red and gray bird sings in

a tree. It is an American robin.

These birds are a sign of spring.

An adult robin is about 9 to 11 inches (23 to 28 centimeters) long. It has a white ring around each eye. Its four toes help it perch.

A hungry robin tugs a worm
from the soil. Gulp!
Robins eat worms and insects.
They also eat fruit in winter.

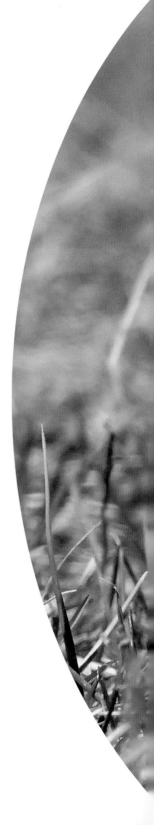

Where Robins Live

American robins live
all over North America.
They live in cities, forests,
fields, and mountains.

Robins migrate south in fall. They go north in spring to breed. Robins travel in flocks.

The Life of a Robin

A female robin builds a nest
of twigs, mud, and grass.

She lays three to five blue eggs.

She sits on the eggs to keep
them warm.

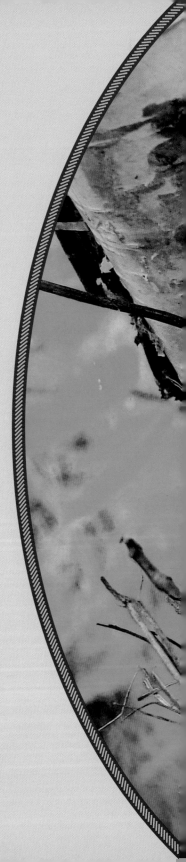

The chicks hatch in about two weeks. Their parents feed them 35 to 40 meals per day. The chicks grow fast. They leave the nest in less than two weeks.

Cats, snakes, and large birds will eat robins and their eggs. Robins screech and dive at the animals. Robins try to keep their young safe.

Robins are fun to watch.

Look for robins in your backyard!

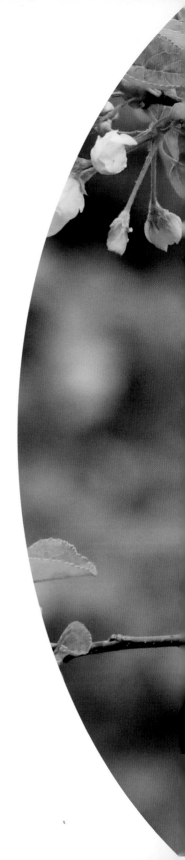

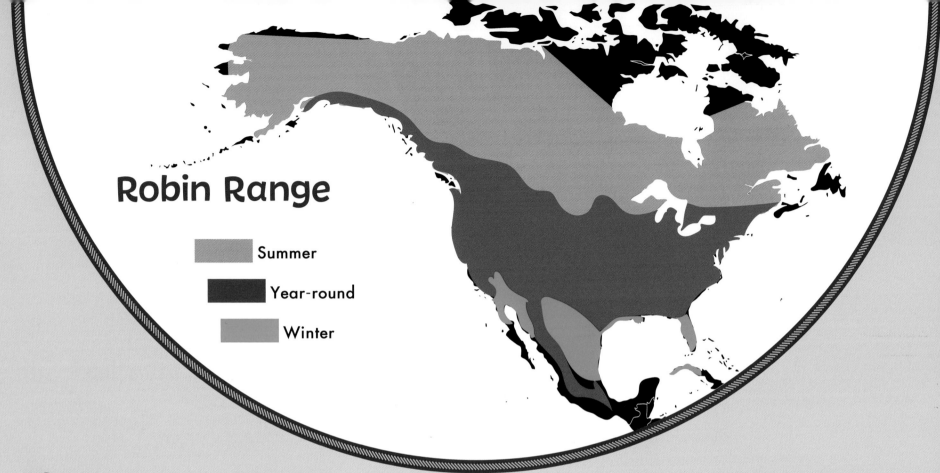

Robin Range

- Summer
- Year-round
- Winter

Glossary

breed—when animals breed, they mate and produce young

chick—a young bird

flock—a group of animals that live, travel, and eat together

hatch—to break out of an egg

migrate—to move from one place to another

nest—a place to lay eggs and bring up young

perch—to sit or stand on a branch or on the edge of something, often high up

Read More

Hudak, Heather C. *Robins: Watch Them Grow*. New York: Weigl Publishers Inc., 2011.

Peterson, Megan Cooley. *Look Inside a Robin's Nest*. Mankato, Minn.: Capstone Press, 2012.

Russo, Monica. *Birdology: 30 Activities and Observations for Exploring the World of Birds*. Chicago: Chicago Review Press, 2015.

Internet Sites

FactHound offers a safe, fun way to find Internet sites related to this book. All of the sites on FactHound have been researched by our staff.

Here's all you do:

Visit *www.facthound.com*

Type in this code: 9781491461105

Super-cool stuff! Check out projects, games and lots more at **www.capstonekids.com**

Critical Thinking
Using the Common Core

1. How many meals does a robin chick eat in one day? (Key Ideas and Details)

2. Do robins live in the same place year round? (Key Ideas and Details)

3. Look at the photo on page 19. Why does the robin fly at the bigger bird? (Integration of Knowledge and Ideas)

Index

Word Count: 196
Grade: 1
Early-Intervention Level: 13